# UNDERSTANDING PRAYER

*DISCOVER THE DIFFERENCE BETWEEN:*

*A PRAY-ER, A PRAYER WARRIOR AND AN*

*INTERCESSOR*

*SHARON MOWERY*

1

Connect With Me!

http://www.thelimpingwriter.com

# DEDICATION

To Jack

I will love you, forever and always.

# SPECIAL THANKS TO

Ramona Mullet

I am grateful for your help.

# TABLE OF CONTENTS

# INTRODUCTION

There have been writers over the centuries who've not done away with the box altogether but who have dared to step right outside the restraints of the box and write.

Writers such as, Audrey Niffenegger, The Time Traveler's Wife //Hilary Mantel, Wolf Hall // John Banville, The Sea // Robert Goolrick, A Reliable Wife // Alice Sebold, The Lovely Bones.

This information was taken from the following website: https://writeitsideways.com/6-writers-who-broke-the-rules-and-got-away-with-it/

My name and book title may never land on a website showing an example of writing outside the box or breaking the rules but in this book I've done just that. This is a nonfiction piece of work. All of the content is true down to the very emotions with which it is written. In this time in our history, the way we "feel" is on the forefront of all we are about. E-motions are the rave. We don't write on Facebook or send an email without inserting a smiley or frownie face. I've chosen to include my emotions in the writing of this book. As the author, I'm not telling you how to react, I'm merely expressing how I feel or felt when the incident happened and am expressing my thoughts or emotions. So yep, I'm breaking the rules in this one! (wink)

# WHAT AM I?

Am I considered a person of prayer?

Do others see me as a prayer warrior?

Or am I an intercessor?

If you've ever asked yourself these questions, then

this book is for you.

Most likely you'll find yourself identifying closer to

one of these areas of prayer.

We'll take a brief look at all three areas,

but the main focus will be on that of

The Intercessor.

# CHAPTER 1

In the following pages I will give you an opportunity to be offended...seriously, I will. But please don't be. It's not my intent to do so. When we're intimidated by someone, or have a lack of self-confidence, someone will say or do something and we may immediately be offended. Instead we should take those words or actions to the Throne and ask God for His help to work through and understand what was meant. It's my personal plea to you; please don't be offended. I mean nothing degrading or derogatory in any way, to anyone.

I dare not say, my experience and knowledge on the subject of prayer is that of a cookie cutter or is all inclusive. All I can speak about is my journey. Yours may look completely different. We may never cross paths, but when we arrive at the destination...we will not need to speak a word. We'll look at one another and know we each counted the cost laid out before us, found it worthy of the price and now, here we are.

We need to stop comparing ourselves to others and stop feeling inadequate. Instead we need to take up our mantle and learn to draw from one another's giftings and strengths. When we do that, together we arrive at the foot of God, in prayer, in unity and in strength.

When I was in my late teens I went through a time where I hungered for God. It was then I began learning about fasting and extended times of (alone) prayer. I remember my first attempt at fasting. I made it until 11:30 at night and gave in for a peanut butter sandwich! Another failed attempt was over fish sticks, and I don't even like fish! Ha, ha, ha.

When I was in my twenties, I married and moved to a different city. I began going to an Assembly of God church. I'm not pushing Assembly of God churches. God will be where hungry and open hearts are no matter the title. But I began learning and growing in spiritual areas.

I remember one night at church, we had gathered at the alter area to worship and pray before dismissing. I

11

was standing next to a lady and she began to cry. As she cried, I began to feel a stirring within my stomach. In a few minutes, I began to cry, and cry and cry. I had no idea why.

I still hadn't heard of or learned about intercession so this experience was new to me. During the following week, a couple from church invited me for coffee. I was telling them about the incident and without hesitation the husband said, "sounds like intercession to me."

They began to explain to me in depth about the act of intercession. I was amazed by the fact that we, mere humans, could be used by God to change a situation or person by tapping into the spiritual realm. God

Himself invites us to partner with Him to accomplish His intended purpose. Wow!

The next thing I remember about the early days of learning about intercession, I was visiting a church to hear the guest speaker. At some point people had gone up for prayer. I remember three children standing together, they were siblings. I don't recall if we were told what the prayer need was.

I was sitting in my seat several rows back and I began to weep. The pastor came to me and asked why I was crying. I told him I didn't know, but it must have something to do with those children. He asked me if I would go to them and join with those who were praying over the children.

I didn't know it then, but I had gone into intercession for those children. I had yet to learn about pressing into God and hearing His heart or receiving understanding from Him about the burden I was receiving. I did what I knew to do, give in to the weeping and allow God to cry over these children for as long as He wanted to.

Not long after this, the church I was attending planned a mission trip to Mexico. The desire to go never entered my mind. As we were leaving church there was a table for sign ups. My husband looked at me and said, "well, go sign up." I'm sure I gave him a questioning look but I signed up.

It was on this mission trip God Himself began expounding on prayer and even showed me through demonstration and His Word, layers in prayer that I'd never realized were there.

By this time, I'd gotten a little better at fasting. I learned not to have peanut butter or fish sticks in the house during a fast! Ha, ha, ha. Just kidding. But glean any wisdom you need to from that statement. *(smile)*

Before the mission trip to Mexico we learned about the area we were going to and different opportunities to minister. I was still very new to the ways of the Assembly of God church. This wasn't the denomination I grew up in.

As time to go to Mexico neared, my excitement grew and I fasted for five WHOLE days, ha, ha, ha. BAM! I will say, I actually thought I might die a couple times during the five days, but as is apparent, I didn't!

There were a few of us that wanted to be a clown and go to a remote area and minister to children. As I prepared through prayer and fasting my heart began to ache to get to those children. Time came and we went. It was incredible. Since I'd never been on a mission trip I had no expectation of what would happen. On day one part of the team gathered and loaded up to go to the dump to minister, some to the downtown area and then my group went to the children. The experiences along the way will have to come out in another book, for now I want to keep my focus on "prayer."

We were only going to be able to go to this remote location once, but we were contacted and told we could go the next day as well. I was beyond excited! The next day, I got up, put my clown make-up on and I felt a sensation I had never felt before. Then I literally thought I heard God speak to me! I heard God say, "don't go today. Stay here with Me." Again, I was new to this and tried to brush off what was happening. I didn't want to stay back. I wanted to go. I began to cry and even though I didn't understand, I knew I needed to tell my mission leader. We talked for a few minutes and I was allowed to stay at the compound.

I spent a few minutes crying over my disappointment which I've since learned is an okay thing to do, but once I got that out, I went outside with my Bible and pen and paper, sat down and for the first time ever I began to commune with God in a personal way. It was an incredible experience. I felt impressed to turn to certain passages of the Bible and I would turn there

17

and as I read the Words, my heart melted and tears fell.

God led me to *Mark 14:32-36*, and as I read this portion of scripture, He would interrupt me (yeah, can you believe God does that? He'll just interrupt you anytime He wants. Ha, ha, ha. I didn't know….).He would stop me and teach me, have me reread what I'd just read and then open my eyes to the layers of meaning and layers of prayer that are there, in plain sight. Even though I was becoming a student of the Bible and was sure I'd read this portion of scripture, I'd never seen what He was showing me then.

You can lay this book down and read these verses in context and come back if you want to. I'm picking up *Mark 14 in verse 32.*

> ³² *And they came to a place which was named Gethsemane: and he saith to his disciples, Sit ye here, while I shall pray.*

> ³³ *And he taketh with him Peter and James and John, and began to be sore amazed, and to be very heavy;*

> ³⁴ *And saith unto them, My soul is exceeding sorrowful unto death: tarry ye here, and watch.*

> ³⁵ *And he went forward a little, and fell on the ground, and prayed that, if it were possible, the hour might pass from him.*

*36 And he said, Abba, Father, all things are possible unto thee; take away this cup from me: nevertheless not what I will, but what thou wilt.*

What the Lord showed me from this portion of scriptures is: There will be times you can surround yourself with others for prayer such as  prayer groups (other pray-ers) to pray for specific people or situations as in v. 32.

There will be times only a select few will be entrusted with details and called upon to engage in prayer with you.  "Crisis Situations" as in v. 33-34 (prayer warriors). In any type of engagement you may want to, or need to, enlist others. None of us is an Island.

Then there will be times where you will be drawn to go into prayer alone, these times are dependant on your availing yourself to the Holy Spirit and could be for an extended period of time. (intercession) as in v. 35-36.

Just as the Trinity is Three-In-One and yet can function separately, so these three types of prayer are in us. Yet one of these areas of prayer is usually more dominate than the other. Another way to say this is: one way of praying will appeal to you while another area of prayer may not. Prayer is nothing more than having dialog with the Lord. As we allow a natural flow to take place we realize it's just like a relationship. Sometimes one person will talk and other times, the other person will. Then there are times you just enjoy being together. Talk isn't always necessary. We don't need to be intimidated by someone else's relationship with prayer nor do we need to feel overwhelmed or inadequate. If you pray, you can tap into all three of these areas of prayer.

We all intercede. The moment you bow your heart or head in prayer, you are interceding.

All prayer, prayed in faith is effective!

The position is determined by the sacrifice.

# CHAPTER 2

Let's examine the difference between what I call:

A Pray-er

A Prayer Warrior

An Intercessor

**A) <u>A pray-er:</u>** *Webster's New World College Dictionary:*

> One that prays. To entreat, make a request or
>
> plea in a humble manner. To address God.

This person(s) can be counted on for daily prayer. They typically use a list or accept requests of prayer from others. They are faithful to their station of prayer. Pray-ers are great at leading or being a part of a "Prayer Chain" type of praying. They are great at collecting prayer requests or being called to be added to a list. Because pray-ers do spend time with God, it may or may not be their preferred way, but they can close themselves off for a time of prayer. They must be careful to not use the same prayer for different needs. When in public they need to be careful not to flaunt phrases or words the Holy Spirit has given them while praying. They should learn how to pray in humility, in private as well as in public, always seeking the heart of God for each individual or prayer need.

*5 And when you pray, you should not be as the hypocrites are: for they love to pray standing in the synagogues and in the corners of the streets, that they may be seen of men. Verily I say unto you, They have their reward.*

*6 But thou, when you pray, enter into thy closet, and when thou hast shut thy door, pray to thy Father which is in secret; and thy Father which sees in secret shall reward thee openly.*

*7 But when ye pray, use not vain repetitions, as the heathen do: for they think that they shall be heard for their much speaking.*

*⁸ Be not ye therefore like unto them: for your Father knows what things ye have need of, before ye ask him.*

*Acts 12-12b-16* is an example of a group of people gathered to pray for a specific thing, in this case Peter, who had been imprisoned. Their prayer was answered. Before we get over into judgment, can we remember praying along side the Holy Ghost and seeing results was a new thing? The girl opening the door was so overwhelmed with joy that she left Peter outside and ran in to tell the others who were still praying. Her report met with opposition but she persisted and finally they went to see for themselves. They too were overcome.

Persons of prayer may not start out praying with full confidence but will grow in their expectation and belief as they see more and more prayers answered. If you find this area of praying effective for you, do not overlook the power of agreement. Find someone with whom you can meet, either in person or over the phone if need be, on a regular basis to pray for specific people or situations. The unity of two praying (Deut. 32:30) can put 10,000 to flight! Do not underestimate the power in prevailing prayer available to you.

**B) <u>Prayer Warrior:</u>** *Webster's New World College Dictionary:*

> A person(s) engaged in a struggle or conflict. A person experienced in warfare such as in the military. Actively engaging in an operation that weakens or destroys another. One in a struggle between competing entities. Often releasing a "war-cry" releasing spiritual forces.

This person(s) is able to immediately activate spiritual forces, recognize and push back darkness (evil) from a situation.

Prayer Warriors are those called on in a crisis situation. They are versed in God's Word to the point they are able to identify and release God's will and Word into or over a situation.

Prayer Warriors are effective in praying on assignment. They don't have to, but are comfortable having contact with the person for whom they're praying. They are eager to sign up for or release a prayer strategy they feel the Holy Spirit has impressed on them. A Prayer Warrior can join in a group setting but can also pray alone. Prayer Warriors love worship music and often engage in warfare during worship. They don't just pray and move on. Once something enters their spirit, they pray with intensity until the burden has lifted.

**C) <u>Intercessor:</u> *Webster's New World College Dictionary:***

A person who intercedes; a mediator

A "go-between"

Intercession may or may not contain words.

<u>**Intercede:**</u> *Webster's New World College Dictionary:*

to plead or make a request in behalf of another or others: to ***intercede*** with the authorities for the prisoner to intervene for the purpose of producing agreement; mediate to make a ***supplication to God*** in behalf of someone: said of a saint so petitioned in prayer

Another definition of intercede is to get involved in something on behalf of another person, or to speak up for or act on someone's behalf. When you get involved in an argument such as that of a lawyer, or stand up for a friend, these are examples of situations where you intercede. But this is not intercession.

So to say again, anytime you pray you ARE interceding even as you pray for yourself.

Persons giving themselves to prayer / intercession will oft times feel compelled to get away from everyone and everything for prayer. As you learn how to identify this urging, you'll begin to recognize it building within yourself. There have been times I would feel a swelling or a rising up within myself and from the deep place within myself, where deep calls to deep, intercession started no matter where I was or who I was with.

I'm not saying you lose all control of your body, but what I am saying is you can literally be so yielded to the Holy Spirit that He overtakes you. And while you are being drawn into intercession, you learn how to withdraw (quickly) and find a place to intercede.

Allow me to say again, intercession may or may not contain words. One form of intercession is expressed through weeping. I use the term weeping because there are times I out-right CRY, but there are times a stream of tears come out of my heart and the emotions associated with weeping are different than those of emotional crying.

We see a distinction in *Malachi 2:13:*

> *V13. and this is the second thing you do: You cover the altar of the Lord with tears, with weeping and crying.....*

Intercessors prevail in prayer until they have an inter-session (Inner-Session) with God and enter deep places in the spiritual realm where they see and hear and feel God's heart. There have been times of intercession where I would be so burdened and as I yielded, all I could do was groan and cry sometimes to the point of travail, or inner agony.

Intercessors might have dreams and visions and prophetic encounters for upcoming events and at times will have been praying for days, weeks, months or even years before information is disclosed to the public.

*Amos 3:7* **Surely the Lord G**ᴏᴅ **will do nothing, but he reveals His secret unto His servants the prophets.**

Oft times intercessors are sent ahead (spiritually speaking) to begin to plow the ground, spy out the land, uncover Gods intent as well as the enemy's strategies. (Joshua and Caleb)

*Numbers 13:1-2, 17-21* **And the L**ᴏʀᴅ **spoke unto Moses, saying,**

**2 Send thou men, that they may search the land of Canaan**

**17 And Moses sent them to spy out the land of Canaan, and said unto them, Get you up this way southward, and go up into the mountain:**

35

*18 And see the land, what it is, and the people that dwells therein, whether they be strong or weak, few or many;*

*19 And what the land is that they dwell in, whether it be good or bad; and what cities they be that they dwell in, whether in tents, or in strong holds;*

*20 And what the land is, whether it be fat or lean, whether there be wood therein, or not. And be ye of good courage, and bring of the fruit of the land. Now the time was the time of the first-ripe grapes.*

*21 So they went up, and searched the land....*

God's intent is for us to grow. It's also God's intent for us to serve out of His Love in prayer for others. We aren't limited. We can grow and learn to flow from one area of prayer to another depending on the need or situation.

*1 Corinthians 13:11* [11] *When I was a child, I spake as a child, I understood as a child, I thought as a child: but when I became a man, I put away childish things.*

*Luke 22:32b Jesus speaking to Peter*

[32] *and when thou art converted, strengthen thy brethren.*

# CHAPTER 3

We are to desire to grow and expand our <u>up-reach</u> as well as our <u>outreach</u>!

As we grow in our relationship with Jesus, we welcome times of intimacy in prayer. Out of those times, in whatever area of prayer we function in, we should begin to see a death to:

The Love of Money; True disciples are givers not hoarders!

Personal Ambition; True disciples seek first the Kingdom of God.

Natural affection for loved ones; True disciples set their mind on eternity and learn how to fully release loved ones to Gods care.

Appetites of the body; True disciples learn discipline.

Love of life itself; True disciples come to a place where they too can say, "To live is Christ, and to die is gain." (*Philippians 1:21*), and are willing to lay down their life for a friend. *(John 15:13)*

> Gal 2:20  I have been crucified with Christ; it is no longer I who live, but Christ lives in me; and the life which I now live in the flesh I live by faith in the Son of God who loved me and gave Himself for me.

The more we allow crucifixion, the deeper in intercession we are taken. We begin to take on the identity of Christ. We identify with Him. Moses' identity began to change while he was still in the palace. He began to identify with his brethren who were slaves but he soon realized he couldn't hang onto the palace life. There had to be a death to his past, and even though Moses didn't know it, the moment he chose to leave the past behind, he began walking toward being the redeemer for his people. There is always a price to pay. A cost to count.

The apostle Paul in Romans 8 and Romans 9 identifies with the gentiles.

Isaiah walks for three years, naked and barefoot

Hosea marries a harlot

Jeremiah isn't allowed to marry

Ezekiel isn't allowed to morn his wife

The more we take on the identity of Christ, the more we will be given opportunity to walk out the inward calling. Christ says in John 5:30b   I do not seek My own will but the will of the Father who sent Me.

There is a place of personal agony in dying to self. We need to allow this process.

> John 12:24-26 ...unless a grain of wheat fall into the ground and dies, it remains alone; but if it dies, it produces much grain. He who loves his life will lose it, and he who hates his life in

this world will keep it for eternal life. If anyone

serves Me, let him follow Me....

We do have a choice. We can be like someone on

oxygen, so attached to this world that we cling to its

support. Letting go of dreams or ambitions can be

bitter sweet. We're growing in the Word and in prayer

and desiring to go deeper. Then the Holy Spirit puts

His finger on something in our life and asks, "May I

have that?" In our infant stage, we are yet to learn,

anything God asks for will be replaced by something

far greater than what we could ever imagine and will

far outweigh in value the thing to which we're

clinging.

So as we begin the dying process, or we see others starting out, let us allow the process to work. *James 1:4 tells us; Let patience have its perfect work.* Allow time for the falling of the corn, allow time for the death of the kernel, allow for the barren-dormant time. Let's not forget our own struggle in the surrender of death, instead let us turn and intercede and encourage one another in God's love.

It is a direct result of growing comfortable (not complacent) but comfortable with extended intimate times with just you and God. The more we're willing to close the door on the world and draw away with God, the more of His love He imparts to us and the more of His secrets He begins to share with us. *(Daniel*

*2:28a) (Amos 3:7)* Can you hear Him now, whispering to you..."Now don't tell anyone I told you this, it's a secret but...!" (smile) Can you just imagine it? It really happens!

After our surrender and death in an area there always comes a breaking of the ground! A visible manifestation of life, of survival! A time of celebration, a time of gift giving which we soon learn, the gift is to be entrusted with a burden for another soul, or people or nation. A burden given to us from God Himself, a weighty matter, not a prayer request given to us from Aunt Suzie or Uncle Harry but a burden that comes to us from the heart of God.

As we carry the burden into intercession, we're no longer thinking about our own self or our own little space but we begin thinking, and moving with Kingdom principles into a place of prayer and intercession in a level of authority that could only come through times of intimacy with Jesus which results in a death to self.

As you yield to, and begin to take on the identity of Christ, others will recognize the place of closeness you walk with Him and they will entreat you to carry their burden. It's sad to say but true, that a lot of times people don't pray. They talk like they do but let them come across someone who carries an anointing in prayer and they are more than willing to hand you their prayer list.

The following is a true account. Before you read it, please allow me to ask for mercy and even some grace. I thought about taking this out but just in case there's another like me out there with such an innocent zeal as well as the ability to make blatant mistakes that you're tempted to react this way, it's for you that I confess to the following account. I have since learned there are more tactful ways of reacting. That I will leave up to you to discover. All I offer is, the way I reacted may not have been the best way. Okay on to the story.

I vividly remember a time I refused a burden of prayer from someone. (For real! I did.) I was standing in the foyer of my church and a man from the congregation came over and started talking to me. Within a few sentences he communicated his prayer list and asked me to also pray. I immediately responded, "No." (Oh my!) I honestly don't remember the prayer request but I do remember we were both shocked at my response. I'd never responded this way before to a prayer request but I thought it was the Holy Spirit. (God is a jealous God. Isn't that a great excuse to pull in right here? Ha, ha, ha.) I went on to tell him to pray and ask God to burden me or others to pray for his requests and if God lead me, I most definitely would pray.

I will admit, I'm (on purpose) very guarded about telling anyone, "Oh sure honey, I'll pray for you." No, I can't say that unless I get an automatic green light from the Holy Spirit as we are speaking. Otherwise, I usually reply, "I'll try to remember. Would you help me by asking God to lay you or your situation on my heart and then of course, I'll join you in prayer." Telling anyone I will pray and then not praying is a serious matter to me. Whether this person prays or not is beside the point. The point is, if you agree to pray for them, they are to some degree counting on your prayer. So some may feel I didn't handle the situation with sensitivity but believe it when I say, my heart was right.

This has also become a comfort to me. There have been times God has dropped someone on my heart and I've covered them in prayer until I felt a release, so I'm sure God does the same on my behalf.

As an intercessor, I don't feel I have the liberty to create my own prayer list. Of course there are people and things I pray for on a regular basis, but I'm talking about the times in intimate fellowship where I'm availing myself to God. He knows far better than I do where the urgency lies. I don't want to be praying for "John Smith" when it's another person or a nation in a critical situation and in dire need of prayer at that moment. Only God has a world's eye view. Therefore, I think it best to get the majority of prayer orders from Him.

Speaking of praying for a nation, I remember the first time I felt burdened to pray for a nation. I can't recall what nation it was, but I was preparing to go on my second missions trip. No matter what other things I attempted to pray for, it was this nation that kept pressing in on me. Yep, here again, God was interrupting my praying! Ha, ha, ha. So I gave in and made this nation a matter of my prayer time.

The missions team went to Mexico again but to a different region. The morning after we arrived, we were introduced to our interpreter. Would you like to guess where he was from? You got it, he was from the nation I'd been praying for! May I tell you, I was blown away. I remember saying to him in an amazed voice, "I've been praying for you!" He gave me one of those half smiles. Unimpressed. But I felt as if a bomb had ignited inside me. God had began using ME to pray. It would be later in the trip before I realized the significance of my obedience to pray prior to the trip, but it made a lasting impression on me.

During this time God expanded my ability to hear and see in the spirit. I realized there was much I didn't yet comprehend and some things *I just knew* were revelations from God that turned out not to be. Even with that confession (to you right now because God already knew I got it wrong), in His mercy and do I dare say, His joy in watching as I eagerly approached Him, God also began opening my understanding.

That was years ago and I still perceive things wrong at times but I can count on that same mercy of God to continue pulling me into the fullness of His truth in revelations He shares with me as I press into Him

Prayer is our lifeline! How incredible it is to be able to talk to God! I mean really, think about it! No wonder we find the term *"Selah"* in the Psalms. When we stop and think about the wonder of An Almighty God and the frailty of man, and that this Holy God invites us to have a relationship and open dialog with Him, what word is there to describe this? *SELAH!*

We should never reach the point where we forget that this "God" we're speaking to is a HOLY GOD nor should we forget the high price GOD paid that enables us to come before Him. Jesus, God's only Son, laid down His life that you and I could at any time, lift our voice and cry out to Him.

God forgive me, forgive us, if we lose our humility in coming before you.

I pray for the "trembling before God's Word" to rise up within us again. I don't disagree with the salutation of *daddy* or *poppa* that I hear as some address God. The fellowship we have with God is a result of our relationship and knowing we ARE loved beyond our comprehension. It's about knowing we are accepted and forgiven, not condemned, and it's about knowing and truly grasping that we Are the righteousness of God. But let us not forget all of the above comes because HE FIRST LOVED US. The closer we get to God and the more we realize the depth of that statement, the more it should humble us.

The position of prayer for any of us depends on how much we're willing to die to self and live in such a way that others see it is Christ that liveth in me. *(Galatians 2:20)* Paul states in 1st Corinthians 15:31 "I die daily." To read this and take it literally would mean that at some point Paul resurrected (his old man). How else could he die again and again, day after day? No! I believe Paul is stating that he looks death in the face every day and in light of a future resurrection, he chooses to risk death. He chooses to run the race and press toward the finish line. He's gained such a place of fellowship with the God Head, that nothing holds a higher place than to live as a walking dead man.

The question is....

How much are you willing to decrease,

That HE may increase?

# PART 2

# CHAPTER 4

I want to give you my testimony. I didn't know much about prayer in relation to prayer actually being a vibrant part of a relationship, and I certainly didn't know how to pray. I'd never heard the word "intercession" and definitely didn't set myself on a course to be an Intercessor. What I did, however, was remain overwhelmed by what Jesus Christ did in me one particular Sunday at church. I was delivered from so much garbage I'd been carrying around for years and I suddenly loved Him with a love that could not be satisfied. It was a glorious, fabulous day! Now it is my hope your faith in and hunger for prayer will increase as I take you with me on my journey to the heart of God. These stories are true encounters, and in retelling them I am once again ignited to run away to the secret place with Him. (warm smile)

I'd known His love when I walked with Him in my teens but this was different. His presence was tangible and I spent every free minute I could sitting at His feet. I devoured the Bible yet when I closed myself off, there were no words, only worship and weeping to the lover of my soul. Words were not needed. We would just spend time together. I could picture myself sitting at His feet with my head on His lap. I'd imagine Him with His hand on my head. I could actually feel Him smile down on me. And so we sat and adored one another.

Earlier in my life, I'd sought God for the infilling of the Holy Ghost. I wanted it now more than ever. I began reading all the material I could get my hands on and began praying that God would baptize me and fill me to overflowing. I was standing in my kitchen one Sunday afternoon and I felt Him pour Himself onto me and I just knew He was going to give it to me at church that night. I was pumped! My faith soared and sure enough He poured His spirit onto and into me that night until I couldn't contain Him and a language came up out of my belly. Talk about getting high. I felt such a sense of affirmation. God had imparted His Spirit to me....to ME!

This season of adoration lasted several months. I read in Genesis how God would go down to the garden in the cool of the day and meet up with Adam and the two of them would walk and talk. An intimate vision of this grew inside my heart until I began desiring that same visitation. If God isn't a respecter of persons, *(Acts 10:34)* then I didn't know why I couldn't walk and talk with God in the same way?

I don't know what I thought God and I had to talk about but I wanted that closeness. I wanted to be His friend, His companion. I began to imagine He was excited and somewhere in heaven He'd watch the clock and wait for the hour for our visit. But little did I know what I was asking for. God did begin to visit me and it was soon apparent, when God speaks He doesn't just chit-chat. As He spoke, it was with words that held the wisdom of the ages. His voice came still and small and yet as boisterous as the sound of many waters. I grabbed a pencil and some paper and tried to write words to convey the meaning. His voice came from deep within and with words not common to me.

I called a lady from my church and read her what I'd written down. She said, "Sharon, that's prophecy!" I was humbled that God would trust me and speak His heart to me. From that day on, I began learning how to hear God's voice. His was a voice unlike any other and, for me, I had little trouble knowing it was Him. God began sharing more and more words of prophecy, words of affirmation and exhortation to His body through me.

Let me stop and interject, God is no respecter of persons. He doesn't love me more than He loves you. He speaks to all of His children, nudging us, inviting us to enter His chambers. The more you sneak away and just enjoy being with Him, the more of His presence will linger as you leave your time with Him and others will sense this on you. So go...go away with Him. Leave your "to do" list and your "woe is me" complaints and just go into Him. Spend time getting to know Him, not just as GOD but as your Father, and before long you too will be saying, "O taste and see that the Lord is good!" *(Psalm 34:8)*

\*\*\*\*\*\*\*\*\*\*\*\*\*\*\*\*\*\*\*\*

Another way God shared His heart for others with me was through touch. There would be times, I would put my hand on someone's shoulder or shake their hand or some other gesture of touch and as my hand was on the individual, I would see God's heart for them. One individual played the guitar in the church band. I don't remember how it happened but I remember putting my hand on him and seeing him in one-on-one situations speaking to people about Christ. I withdrew my hand and told him what I had envisioned. He looked at me like a deer in headlights.

Later in the church service, he testified, which is something he never did. He testified about what was spoken to him. He never mentioned my name.

His voice trembled and he fought tears as he shared the message and confirmed his desire to win those he worked with to the Lord. His wife came to me later and told me she'd never seen her husband so moved that he would actually cry. God had revealed and confirmed the secrets of his heart to him.

*********************

I recall in the 90's the church went through a time of engaging in "warfare praying." This kind of forceful attacking of the enemy appealed to me. I was eager to participate in any type of praying. I was learning and felt empowered when I gathered with others. The gathering would usually start with energetic music and no one in the room seemed intimidated by anyone else. There was walking and laying on the ground. There was crying out and declaring God's Word.

Usually it would last a couple hours until everyone was exhausted.

I found myself engaging in this type of boisterous praying even at home. I do dare admit, it was as emotional as it was effective. But may I be given grace here and say again, I was just learning. It was on my second mission trip God helped me realize the source of power. I'd went outback on the compound we were staying at, and there was a dim streetlight in the far corner of the grounds. Other than that it was dark. I was sitting outback and in the spirit, I saw these little gremlin like creatures hopping towards the concreted area. They stopped right at the edge as if they knew better than to get into the light. I felt my inner self begin to rise up with a warfare cry but as soon as it did, I heard the Lord say, "No. Speak to them in My

Name and they will have to go." What! (Again, the Lord is interrupting me!) Ha, ha, ha. I sat there trying to decipher the message. He repeated the Words. "Speak to them in My Name and they will have to go." He wasn't allowing me to physically engage, instead He was showing me the power to dispel darkness and demons comes from Him and His redemptive work and not my works of the flesh even though I was doing them in what I thought was prayer.

This incident would forever change the way I prayed, as well as cause me to make sure it was the power source of Jesus Christ and not my own I was tapping into. Only He has the power to change anything or anyone! No amount of screaming or yelling will change anything other than cause us to become hoarse.

********************

It was on this same mission trip (the second one I'd gone on), and we were returning to Mexico. We were following the same route but our destination was a different region. There were about thirty of us on the bus. We'd been singing and praising and worshiping. I sensed a stirring and took out a pen and paper and wrote down a message and gave it to the mission leader. The Lord said a few things to us as a group but the one thing we didn't understand until we were sitting at the border was, "You will go in, but you will go in a different way."

When we arrived at the border crossing we weren't allowed to enter the country of Mexico. We had picked up a man who would be traveling with us and when we were allowed to leave this gentleman took us into Mexico but we went in a different way than we had our last trip!! God was showing us beforehand so when we encountered opposition we wouldn't worry but would trust Him. The more God spoke to me and through me, the more sure of His voice I became, and the more confident I became to step out and deliver the message.

*******************

There was another time at church when we were gathered around the alter and I looked over at a lady. I felt strongly I needed to go speak to her. I opened my mouth and for the next few minutes I spoke a message to her I had no intention of speaking. She began to cry. When I finished, she said she'd written a letter to a friend she was taking to the airport. The letter spoke of her secret love for them but she didn't give it to them. Everything I said to her was what she'd put in the letter. As I spoke, she realized it was a message to her and not to her friend. God had her write her own love letter from Him to her and then revealed it to her through my obedience.

*******************

Want a story that doesn't involve church? (smile) My husband liked to eat the moment his feet hit the floor. On a particular morning I'd gotten up early. I went ahead and prepared breakfast and began some household chores. I heard the Lord say, "Fix his plate and heat it up." I hadn't heard my husband get up but I knew I'd heard the Lord. So I fixed my husband a plate and had it in the microwave. He came down the stairs, and as soon as he walked through the kitchen the microwave dinged. I didn't tell him about the Lord telling me to fix his plate, but set it before him and went on about my chores.

The Holy Spirit is constantly leading us if we'll but yield to Him and believe it is Him speaking, and just obey. There have been a few times I'll see a lady and "know" she's pregnant. I've always told the lady what I discerned and so far God's gotten it right every time. Ha, ha, ha.

\*\*\*\*\*\*\*\*\*\*\*\*\*\*\*\*\*\*\*\*

One Wednesday I'd taken off work to spend the day with my husband because I was going out of town for the weekend. Earlier in the week we had to call a repairman to come to our home and repair a window. We received a call Wednesday morning and they were sending a repairman out that day. I was disappointed. I didn't want to spend the day doing home repairs. I went into the bedroom and prayed and asked God for a Word for this repairman. Since he was interrupting my day at least we could get some ministry in, right?

No sooner had I prayed and the name Judy came to my mind. I didn't know anyone named Judy. I was excited. "Oh boy, here it comes!" I thought. But nothing more came, just the name Judy. I kept listening and listening but nothing was coming. When I knew the repairman was almost done, I went into the front room and waited for him to come through. He did and somehow walked past me. He stopped right outside the door and was talking to my husband. I went over to the doorway and said, "Excuse me, but do you know anyone named Judy?" I still didn't have anything else!!! He said he did and told me who she was. In my desperation I said, "Well, would you tell her..... That was all the Lord was waiting for, my obedience to go with what He'd given me and after I spoke the name Judy the Lord expounded and I uttered a message to Judy from the Lord and asked him to deliver it to her. The Lord spoke a Word of encouragement to her and all three of us standing there were affected.

The repairman was of a religion that didn't operate in the gifts but the Lord gave him "goose-bumps" and he even confessed, it was from the Lord. God wanted to speak to Judy and He did it in such a way the repairman was caught in the crosshairs and couldn't deny it was the workings of the Lord.

I've since then asked the Lord not do that to me anymore but seems He has His own agenda and simply ignores my requests sometimes! Ha, ha, ha.

\*\*\*\*\*\*\*\*\*\*\*\*\*\*\*\*\*\*\*\*

There was a couple in our church. Their faces would pop into my thoughts and I heard the word "MOVE" I hadn't heard them say they were moving or even thinking of moving, and I selfishly didn't want them to move. I was thinking of the word move as a geographic move. I knew they had family in a different state. I didn't withhold the word out of rebellion, I just wasn't sure what it meant so I didn't say anything to them. This went on for two weeks when I finally approached them and said, "the Lord says to tell you guys to MOVE." They looked at one another and then back at me. They'd suffered some financial loss and were struggling to make their house payment. They didn't want to just walk off and lose their house but felt they were to move.

They were waiting for confirmation as to what to do so when I obeyed and spoke the word, they were able to let go and move and get out from under the financial pressure. I was delighted to hear they only moved about five miles from their present location. God will speak to us to confirm something to others. When we do, they will know it's God and the message will be received.

\*\*\*\*\*\*\*\*\*\*\*\*\*\*\*\*\*\*\*

I remember when I was first beginning to tap into the spiritual realm in prayer. I would lay in the floor with soft worship music playing in the background and just allow my mind to be drawn away with the Lord. I didn't resist the pull. This is an account of an encounter I had while laying before the Lord.

I was sitting on a road and on my left was a brilliant green field dotted with boxwood bushes. I stood up and as I did, I was a little girl of about ten years old. I had on a little white dress. My long blond hair was tied back with a white ribbon. I can still see myself looking down at myself and my new dress. I began hearing the sound of someone and looked into the field and I saw a man wearing a long white robe. He was laughing. I will never forget the joy I felt the moment I stepped into the field. I don't know how I knew it, but I knew it was Jesus. He darted around one of the large boxwood bushes, all the while laughing. I took off chasing Him. I watched myself playing hine-and-seek with Jesus. I don't know how long I was there but when I realized I was once again in my own house laying in the floor, I opened my eyes and carried that feeling of joy and peace and innocence and purity throughout the day.

I don't know that I was expecting to, but for a while each day when I laid before the Lord, I would find myself going through this same experience. I sometimes couldn't wait to go away with Him. As much as knowing it was Jesus it was so much more than that. It was a little girl playing with her father. There was nothing hurtful or scary in this place. And no, I don't have a split personality! Ha, ha, ha. But during this time of visiting this place, I not only received healing but I received affirmation of a love so deep and so pure that came from God. I could never be moved out of the mind set that GOD LOVES ME! Oh, yes He does!!

*********************

There came a day however that I laid before the Lord, now expecting to go away with Jesus to this field to play. I once again arrived on this road but when I stood up, I wasn't the little girl, I was present-day me wearing a gray dress that had soiled spots on it and I didn't have on shoes. As I stood up, I remember looking down at my hands and seeing they were dirty. I tried to brush the dust and dirt off. I was puzzled. There was also no sound coming from the field. I heard instead sounds coming from somewhere straight ahead. I looked in the distance I saw this huge room at the end of the road. I started cautiously walking toward it. As I approached, it reminded me of Santa's workshop. Please forgive the analogy but that's what I compared it to. There were little adult people running around like busy bees. I walked into the room and stood in the center slowly turning around as I looked at everything going on. All of the sudden three or four little men ran up to me. They carried a step stool and measuring tape. I wasn't afraid. There was no fear but I was curious as to what was going on. They didn't acknowledge me in any way but set out measuring my arms, my waist, my legs, my feet, they measured every part of me, and then they ran off again. In a few minutes they entered the room again carrying a suit of armor and they carefully placed it on me. The next thing I remember, I opened my eyes and I was once again in my house laying before the Lord, and I knew I'd been given a permanent suit of armor.

*********************

There was a time I was in prayer with another

intercessor. We were sitting outside one evening and

began praying in the Spirit. I sensed we had moved

into the spirit realm and for some reason I stopped

praying. She however continued praying. She would

pray for several seconds, pause and then pray again.

She did this a few times. Start, pause, start, pause.

After what seemed like an hour, but I'm sure it wasn't,

we both felt a release and opened our eyes at the

same time. She looked at me and I told her what I'd

been seeing as she prayed. We had together entered

the Throne Room. We were kneeling before God. He

was sitting in a huge chair. That was all I saw in the

room. As she would pray, God watched her. When she would pause, God would take His right hand, reach behind His chair and bring out a gift and give it to one of us. In one instance, He brought out a large egg. When He did, somehow she knew it was for her. She tilted her head back. He cracked the egg and dropped it into her mouth. He then took a wire whisk like you use in your kitchen when you're cooking, and he whipped the egg. Then she swallowed it. He then said He was giving her the gift of tongues with interpretations. As she again was praying, after she paused, God reached behind His chair and drew out a sword. As He brought it around front of Him, I tilted my head back and He slowly inserted it down my throat. I brought my head back down and looked at Him. He said, I am giving you backbone. You will never bend or bow to the enemy again. Every prayer encounter changed me but this was the first time I'd ever been in the Spirit with someone else.

*******************

Only one other time that I recall has anything like that happened where I had someone else with me. I remember waking up very early one morning. As I laid in the bed I remained still and silent. I could literally smell the smells of war. Smells of gunpowder and dirt and blood. I knew I had awakened to a battle and I attempted to pray. My stomach muscles felt as if I'd been working out for hours. Even though I had just awakened, I knew I'd been fighting a spiritual battle even while I'd been asleep in the natural. I can't explain how this happened, but my daughter who was about seven or eight at the time, was asleep in the next room. I reached through the wall (just like Stretch Armstrong) and took her and laid her on my stomach and she and I began interceding until the next thing I remember I was once again waking up and my daughter wasn't with me. I still have no idea what was going on or for whom we were interceding but I realized no matter how young a person is, if they're born again of the Spirit of God, they are as powerful as any General. It's the same Spirit in all of us, the Spirit of God!

*******************

I recall two lost gentlemen for whom I had been praying. On this particular day, I'd gone for a walk in the country. I began asking God to show me the hindrances coming against these men. I saw both of them standing before God. God had a Bible in his hand. He opened it and began tearing the pages out. He would wad them page by page and put them in one man's mouth until there was no more room. He then went over to the other man and caked his eyes with mud that instantly hardened. The Lord said the first man has had so much religion shoved down his throat that he literally gags when anyone tries to speak to him about his soul. The second man has been so blinded by the hardness of judgment of others that he is no longer able to see anyone genuinely leading him to Christ. Neither of these men had any idea or concept of the battle raging for their souls.

\*\*\*\*\*\*\*\*\*\*\*\*\*\*\*\*\*\*\*\*

Another time in prayer, I could see myself kneeling on the ground in a great expanse of barren dry land. I was crying. My face was streaked with tears and dust. I saw a vast amount of people walking toward me. They were gray and ashen and showed no sign of life. They walked as though they were in a trance. As they passed me, they would fall into a vast opening and every time one of them walked off into the opening, a fume of smoke would ascend. I remember screaming and crying. It was a greater sorrow than I thought I could bear. I don't know how long I literally cried even after this vivid encounter ended. The Lord showed me a few days later the weight of lost souls. Hell enlarges itself everyday. (Isaiah 5:14)  Oh that men everywhere would pray.

\*\*\*\*\*\*\*\*\*\*\*\*\*\*\*\*\*\*\*

I remember sitting on the front row in church and while the pastor was preaching, I began seeing this clear liquid substance being poured on him and then I would see that same clear liquid ascend off him. Don't ask me what he was preaching about because I'd stopped listening to him and was watching what was going on around him in the spirit. I'd never seen this before. It was exciting. As I watched, I don't know how I knew, but I knew this clear substance was the anointing. It would ascend and descend ...on and off. The excitement was replaced with a sternness and with that same "knowing" I knew this man was compromising and the anointing on his life was at stake. I was so bothered by this revelation, it was all I could do to keep sitting there. Did I go to this man and tell him what I had seen? That's confidential. I will say, if you are ever given information such as this, be sure to not release it to ANYONE unless you have a friend or spouse you confide in. God will help you and tell you what you are to do with the revelation, if anything. Perhaps you are to just pray for this pastor or person. Always allow God to lead your revelations.

\*\*\*\*\*\*\*\*\*\*\*\*\*\*\*\*\*\*\*

I have a friend who I'll call "Suzie" (not her real name). Suzie worked for a non-profit organization. Suzie would call me from time to time to pray. One day I'd stopped by to chat with her. She told me there was a lady she'd like me to meet, said she was an intercessor too and would be back in her office next Tuesday. She told me the lady's name and I left. As I drove home, I felt this heaviness wrap itself around me. I imagined it to be like what the Bible calls "gross darkness." I knew it had something to do with this lady I was to meet in a few days. It was strong. I didn't feel a burden to pray and let the whole experience pass. On the morning of the day I was to meet the lady, once again the heaviness returned. I wasn't sure I wanted to meet her but I knew I had to. When I went into the front office of the non-profit building she was standing there. We introduced ourselves and waited for Suzie to finish her phone call so we could go in. I tried to strike up a conversation and find out some details. She was a very lovely lady. From outward appearance she had it all together. When we went into the office, Suzie told us some things that were going on and asked us to join her in prayer. We shut the door and began praying. I knew I wouldn't be able to engage in prayer until we prayed over this lady. I asked her permission and pulled a chair out for her to sit in. As soon as I laid my hand on her shoulder I KNEW what the heaviness was. In her not-so-distant past, even though she loved the Lord with a strong love, she had fallen into sin. It was a brief encounter and even though she'd repented several times, she could not and would not forgive herself. She had brought such a weight of condemnation upon herself and felt she was a martyr, doomed to suffering for her sins. (The enemy of our soul is such a LIAR!) The Holy Spirit did not reveal her sin to me. It was none of my business. Revealing and reaffirming God's love for her and freeing her from condemnation was! (Excuse me for a moment while I do a halleluiah foot shuffle...yep, you caught me...I'm dancing! Ha, ha, ha.) God is so good! Oh how He loves you and me! He loved her too much to leave her to carry a burden His Son died to take away from her.

\*\*\*\*\*\*\*\*\*\*\*\*\*\*\*\*\*\*\*\*

I had the following dream. I was standing on what looked like a stage with a few others looking down onto a construction site. There was nothing but red clay mud and heavy equipment, bulldozers, dump trucks and various other heavy pieces of equipment. The workers were busy clearing the land and removing large boulders as well as other debris. Trucks were going every which way. I saw a family driving onto the property dodging the heavy machinery. About midway in, their car bogged down. The tires sank into the mud and they were stuck. The family got out and climbed on top of the car and were huddled together praying the workers would notice they were there and not run over them. When I woke, I knew this was a warning dream from the Lord but I didn't know this family. The next time I was at church we had a family visiting who were preparing to leave for the mission field. I remember someone calling my name. I turned around and there they stood with the pastor's wife. I don't recall why but I was introduced to them. When I shook their hands, I felt an overwhelming sensation of danger for them. Not quite sure what to do since I didn't know this family nor did they know me, I pulled the pastor's wife aside and told her my dream and told her I didn't think they were supposed to leave yet. Things weren't ready. I don't know if she told them or if they went. I submitted the dream to my leadership and left it there.

\*\*\*\*\*\*\*\*\*\*\*\*\*\*\*\*\*\*\*\*

I remember being in prayer and I was walking in a desert place. There was nothing but dry hot sand and a beaming sun. I don't know how long I'd been walking but my lips were chapped and cracked with visible signs of dried blood. My face was streaked from dried up sweat that had caked with sand and settled on my face. At some point, I fell to the ground from exhaustion and lack of water. When I opened my eyes my head was laying on Jesus' lap. I don't know where He got water from, but He held a sponge over my face and was allowing drips of cold water to fall on my lips. I opened my mouth to receive the water but it wasn't dripping fast enough. I was so thirsty. I reached my hand up to His and tried my best to squeeze His hand tighter around the sponge so the water would come out faster but He wouldn't let me. He said because I was so dehydrated, if He gave me too much, too fast, my body would reject it and I would throw it up and I would be worse off. I had to allow the slow dripping of the water.

*******************

For whatever reason, I once took a job at a funeral home. It was day three and we were taken on a tour of the building, embalming room included. We weren't licensed so we couldn't go in the room but we each looked through the glass plate window on the door. We were shown the insides of the embalming compartment. As I stood looking for what seemed like an eternity, but I'm sure was only a matter of a few seconds, the smell from the inside of that room filled my nose. It was a smell like none other I'd ever smelled and I felt as if I were suffocating. I left for lunch and never returned. I went home and went into prayer. I was going through a very difficult financial period and if I didn't keep this job I wouldn't be able to pay my bills. I was pacing the floor and crying out to God. As I did, a particular nation popped in my spirit. "Are you kidding me God? I need income and You want me to pray for a nation?" I heard that still small voice say, "Seek first the Kingdom of God and all these things will be added to you." (Matthew 6:33) I stopped praying for my needs and interceded for that nation. Later in the evening I got a phone call from a lady I knew. She told me when she was a little girl, there was a man who would give her a nickel every day to buy ice cream from the ice cream truck. She said her family was very poor and she was often hungry. As an adult she realized God had sent this man into her life. She then asked me for permission for her to give me a nickel. The following day was Wednesday, I went to church and she met me, handed me an envelope and told me not to open it until I got home. When I did open it and saw what was in it I called my two children over and we sat down at the table and one by one I pulled out ten, one hundred dollar bills and laid them out for my children to see. I told them, "Trust God, do as He leads and He will provide."

\*\*\*\*\*\*\*\*\*\*\*\*\*\*\*\*\*\*\*\*

I'd just relocated myself and my two children and my finances were tight. I was working but looking for a better paying job. I'd paid the bills for the week and had $3.28 left over. Not much at all but all our needs had been met. It was December and my concern was

Christmas. I was before the Lord and He told me He was sending me $500.00. I had walked with the Lord long enough to believe Him. I was thrilled! I was riding to church with a friend and when she picked me up I told her what the Lord had told me. She handed me an envelope and told me her son and daughter-in-law had given it to her to give to me. I opened it and pulled out a fifty dollar bill. I was pumped!! Here it comes I told her! When the offering was being taken up I thought, I need to pay my tithe on this fifty dollars but felt a bit embarrassed to ask for the change. As I held the fifty dollars in my hand, that still small voice spoke to me again and said, "No, you've gotten it wrong, this is the tithe for the five hundred dollars I'm sending." I know I laughed. My

God is so good to me! Not only was He buying

Christmas, He was paying His own tithe! What a God!!!

\*\*\*\*\*\*\*\*\*\*\*\*\*\*\*\*\*\*\*

I have always had a habit of lingering at the alter.

Everybody else will be up talking about the Super

Bowl or the next best movie coming out and there I'll

be, laying on the alter crying. One such time as I

lingered, I saw the Lord's hand extend and He Himself

invited me to sit at the banquet table. If I had rushed

away, I would have missed out on a personal

invitation.

********************

There was a time I'd given myself to intercede for a particular thing. I'd spend as much time as I could praying. My husband and I would go to bed and I'd lay next to him until I knew he was asleep and then I'd get up and lay in the floor and continue to intercede which brought weeping with it. After a while, I got back into bed and I said, "Lord, I will pray but I need your strength to continue. I'm so physically tired." No sooner had I finished my sentence when I felt His hand, starting at my head, slide down my whole body and He picked me up in His hand and as He did He turned me around so that my feet were at His face. He then began blowing His breath over me, up and down, up and down. I don't know if you've ever seen the old King Kong movie where King Kong has taken the lady captive and he's had her a day or so when he carries her to a waterfall and puts her in the flow of the water. She's not sure at first but then feeling no danger, she relaxes and lets the water refresh her. King Kong then pulls her close to him and blows his breath on her until her hair and clothes are dry. That was what this felt like. I was in God's hand and His breath was blowing over me. He then laid me back down in my bed and withdrew His hand. He was refreshing me and enabling and empowering me to continue in prayer until the victory came.

*********************

I was working in an office building and the executive offices were on the second floor. There was no reason we needed to be on this floor. At times someone from the executive offices would come to our floor for a meeting or some other business. When they did, we had been instructed to continue our work and were not to engage in conversation with them. Well, guess what? One Friday most everyone from my floor had gone to lunch. I caught a glimpse of a man walking around and knew he was from the executive floor. He was walking through the isles looking at people's work stations. When he got to mine he stopped and stood behind me and watched me as I worked. In a minute or so, he asked me my name. I told him, paused and turned around and said, "Since you know my name, I should know yours." He chuckled and told me his name. I turned back around and continued working. In a few seconds he patted my shoulder. When his hand touched my shoulder, I started receiving a revelation about his health. I also saw two adult women standing together holding one another and shuddering with fear. In a few seconds he walked over to the window and stood looking out. The Lord told me to go tell him what I'd seen and to tell him he would be okay, and to also tell his wife and daughter that the Lord says he's going to be okay because they are afraid he's going to die. I took a deep breath and...remained in my seat. I let my fear of the "rules" override my obedience to God.

I had no idea of his position in the company I only knew he was from the executive offices. By the end of the day I was miserable because of my disobedience. I went down to the second floor on my way out and found his office, he was the CEO of the company, but to my disappointment he had gone for the day. All weekend long I covered this man and his family in prayer all the while repenting and telling God I'd go speak to the man first thing Monday morning.

So Monday came and I got off the elevator on the second floor. I was walking toward his office and I saw his secretary approaching me. I couldn't let her stop me. The man's door was open so I slipped in and greeted him. I had seen his secretary standing outside the door with her hands on her hips, but I kept my focus. I asked his permission to speak to him on a non-work related matter. He gave me permission. I shut the door, also with his permission. I recalled the events of Friday when he'd visited our floor. He remembered speaking to me and I proceeded to tell him what the Lord had shown me about his health and his family. He was very touched and stood up pulling one side of his suit jacket back. On his hip hung some sort of machine. He explained that his heart stops beating and the machine would shock his heart and cause it to start beating again. I wasn't glad about his health issue, but I sure was relieved the Lord had given me another chance to obey Him because not only was I blessed, so was the man I was standing before.

*********************

# Conclusion:

Jeremiah 33:3, Call to Me and I will answer you, and show you great and mighty things, which you do not know.

Prayer isn't a mystic happening. Instead it's as real as you sitting where you are at this very moment, reading this material. God loves you! He would love for you to lay aside all the rules and restrictions and just come to Him as you would any other person and "hang out" with Him. Let Him start the conversation. Ask Him what's on His heart. The above verse in Jeremiah tells you, He will SHOW you GREAT and MIGHTY things. Wow! Why would we not be enticed to at least allow Him to fulfill His Word to us? As you do, you will find yourself eager to close yourself off

with Him. He will become your bread and your wine.

# My Prayer For You:

Father, I pray for the person reading this book. Draw them to You with such an unrelenting love that they will not be able to resist You. Send Your Holy Spirit to invade their thoughts. Interrupt them! Break in unexpectedly. Cause them to desire this same place of prayer where they too walk and talk with You. Help them to let go of anything, or any thought pattern that hinders them from coming to You. Even if they do it in secret and feel embarrassed or silly at first. Cause them to sense You, eagerly watching them as they approach You. Send great joy to their heart and engage them in such a way they are forever changed. Amen.

# APPENDIX

I've provided below a partial list of Scriptures for each three areas of prayer for you to read. Most scriptures that apply to one area, can also be said of the others. There are many, many other scriptures in the Bible on prayer. I encourage you to seek these out.

## Pray-er

Proverbs 18:1, 4 Through desire a man, having separated himself, seeketh and intermeddleth with all wisdom.
[4] The words of a man's mouth are as deep waters, and the wellspring of wisdom as a flowing brook.

Isaiah 50:4-5 [4] The Lord God hath given me the tongue of the learned, that I should know how to speak a word in season to him that is weary: he wakeneth morning by morning, he wakeneth mine ear to hear as the learned. [5] The Lord God hath opened mine ear, and I was not rebellious, neither turned away back.

Jeremiah 7:16 [16] Therefore pray not thou for this people, neither lift up cry nor prayer for them, neither make intercession to me: for I will not hear thee.

Jeremiah 14:11, 17 [11] Then said the Lord unto me, Pray not for this people.... [17] Therefore thou shalt say this word unto them; Let mine eyes run down with tears night and day, and let them not cease:

Jeremiah 33:3 <sup>3</sup> Call unto me, and I will answer thee, and show thee great and mighty things, which thou knowest not.

Jeremiah 42:7 <sup>7</sup> And it came to pass after ten days, (of praying) that the word of the Lord came unto Jeremiah.

Daniel 3:13b but (Daniel) maketh his petition three times a day.

1 Timothy 2:1 I exhort therefore, that, first of all, supplications, prayers, intercessions, and giving of thanks, be made for all men;

## Prayer Warrior

Psalm 94:16 <sup>16</sup> Who will rise up for me against the evildoers? or who will stand up for me against the workers of iniquity?

Isaiah 58:1 Cry aloud, spare not, lift up thy voice like a trumpet, and shew my people their transgression, and the house of Jacob their sins.

Jeremiah 31:15-16 <sup>15</sup> Thus saith the LORD; A voice was heard in Ramah, lamentation, and bitter weeping; Rachel weeping for her children refused to be comforted for her children, because they were not. <sup>16</sup> Thus saith the LORD; Refrain thy voice from weeping, and thine eyes from tears: for thy work shall be rewarded, saith the LORD; and they shall come again from the land of the enemy.

Jeremiah 38:21b  this is the word that the LORD hath shewed me:

Jeremiah 51: 20-23  20 Thou art my battle axe and weapons of war: for with thee will I break in pieces the nations, and with thee will I destroy kingdoms; 21 And with thee will I break in pieces the horse and his rider; and with thee will I break in pieces the chariot and his rider; 22 With thee also will I break in pieces man and woman; and with thee will I break in pieces old and young; and with thee will I break in pieces the young man and the maid; 23 I will also break in pieces with thee the shepherd and his flock; and with thee will I break in pieces the husbandman and his yoke of oxen; and with thee will I break in pieces captains and rulers.

Jonah 1:6 <sup>6</sup> So the shipmaster came to him, and said unto him, What meanest thou, O sleeper? arise, call upon thy God, if so be that God will think upon us, that we perish not.

## Intercessor

Isaiah 53:11-12 [11] He shall see of the travail of his soul, and shall be satisfied: by his knowledge shall my righteous servant justify many; for he shall bear their iniquities. [12] Therefore will I divide him a portion with the great, and he shall divide the spoil with the strong; because he hath poured out his soul unto death:

Isaiah 59:16 [16] And he saw that there was no man, and wondered that there was no intercessor:

Jeremiah 7:16 [16] Therefore pray not thou for this people, neither lift up cry nor prayer for them, neither make intercession to me: for I will not hear thee.

Jeremiah 10:19 [19] Woe is me for my hurt! my wound is grievous; but I said, Truly this is a grief, and I must bear it.

Jeremiah 13:17 [17] But if ye will not hear it, my soul shall weep in secret places for your pride; and mine eye shall weep sore, and run down with tears, because the Lord's flock is carried away captive

Jeremiah 27:18 [18] But if they be prophets, and if the word of the Lord be with them, let them now make intercession to the Lord of hosts,

Jeremiah 38:21b  this is the word that the LORD hath shewed me:

Lamentations 2:18-19  18 Their heart cried unto the LORD, O wall of the daughter of Zion, let tears run down like a river day and night: give thyself no rest; let not the apple of thine eye cease. 19 Arise, cry out in the night: in the beginning of the watches pour out thine heart like water before the face of the LORD: lift up thy hands toward him for the life of thy young children, that faint for hunger in the top of every street.

Habakkuk 2:1-3 I will stand upon my watch, and set me upon the tower, and will watch to see what he will say unto me, and what I shall answer when I am reproved. 2 And the LORD answered me, and said, Write the vision, and make it plain upon tables, that he may run that readeth it. [3] For the vision is yet for an appointed time, but at the end it shall speak, and not lie: though it tarry, wait for it; because it will surely come, it will not tarry.

Romans 8:26 [26] Likewise the Spirit also helpeth our infirmities: for we know not what we should pray for as we ought: but the Spirit itself maketh intercession for us with groanings which cannot be uttered.

Romans 11:2a [2] God hath not cast away his people which he foreknew. Wot ye not what the scripture saith of Elias? how he maketh intercession to God....

Hebrews 7:25-26 [25] Wherefore he is able also to save them to the uttermost that come unto God by him, seeing he eve liveth to make intercession for them. [26] For such an high priest became us, who is holy, harmless, undefiled, separate from sinners, and made higher than the heavens;

# About The Author

Sharon Mowery has always loved creating with words. Her first recognized work was a poem she created in junior high school where she won a contest for a bicentennial celebration. It was at that time she realized her passion was more than just a passion but her ability to create with words was a true gift from God.

As with anything we're given, it is up to us to hone our gift to make it presentable to the public.

Sharon is a freelance writer and speaker. Understanding Prayer combines two of Sharon's passions; writing and prayer.

She is available to speak at your event and bring this book to life. You may contact her through her website.

http://www.thelimpingwriter.com

Do drop in for a visit.

# May I Ask?

If you enjoyed this book and found it helpful, I would appreciate if you'd take time out of your day and post a short review on Amazon. Your support really matters and I take the time to read every review. Your feedback will help me create even better works for my readers.

# {SMILE}

Printed in Great Britain
by Amazon